*the*
# LITTLE WAY

*reflections on the joy of smallness in GOD'S infinite love*

*the "little flower"*

## ST. THÉRÈSE OF LISIEUX

W

WHITAKER
HOUSE

The wording of Scripture verses quoted by St. Thérèse from the works cited below has been retained from the original translations (from French to English), with the exception that some words that had been capitalized have been lowercased for consistency with the style used in this book. Bible references to these verses are included in footnotes.

Unless otherwise indicated, all quotations are taken from *Soeur Thérèse of Lisieux, the Little Flower of Jesus: A New and Complete Translation of L'Histoire D'Une Ame, with an Account of Some Favours Attributed to the Intercession of Soeur Thérèse*, ed. T. N. Taylor (London: Burns, Oates & Washbourne, 1922). Public domain. Quotations have been lightly edited for the modern reader for clarity, readability, spelling, punctuation, and capitalization.

Quotations cited as *CLFW* are taken from Rev. Albert H. Dolan, O. Carm., *Collected Little Flower Works* (Chicago: Carmelite Press, 1929).

## THE LITTLE WAY:
reflections on the joy of smallness in GOD's infinite love

ISBN: 978-1-64123-951-6
eBook ISBN: 978-1-64123-952-3
Printed in Colombia
© 2023 by Whitaker House

Whitaker House
1030 Hunt Valley Circle
New Kensington, PA 15068
www.whitakerhouse.com

Library of Congress Control Number: 2022951448

1 2 3 4 5 6 7 8 9 10 11 **WH** 30 29 28 27 26 25 24 23

"I offered myself to our Lord to be His Little Flower; I longed to console Him, to draw as near as possible to the tabernacle, to be looked on, cared for, and gathered by Him."

"In my 'little way,' everything is most ordinary; all that I do, little souls must be able to do likewise."

—St. Thérèse of Lisieux

# Introduction to the Life and Influence of St. Thérèse of Lisieux

St. Thérèse of Lisieux,[1] known as "the Little Flower," was a Discalced Carmelite nun who lived in the late nineteenth century. Although she died in a secluded convent in France at the young age of twenty-four, her renowned spiritual writings have been read by multitudes of people around the world. The town where she lived has reportedly been visited by up to two million Christian pilgrims a year.[2]

Born Marie-Françoise-Thérèse Martin on January 2, 1873, in Alençon, France, Thérèse was the youngest of five surviving children in a close, devout Catholic family. Thérèse's beloved mother died when she was four, devastating her and causing her personality to change from lively and strong-willed to "timid, shy, and extremely sensitive."[3] The family soon moved to Lisieux, France, where Thérèse grew up under the loving nurture of her godly father, older sisters, and aunt and uncle. Yet her grief over her mother's death persisted for years, and, while her dedication

---

1. St. Thérèse's official religious name is "Teresa of the Child Jesus and the Holy Face."
2. Mary Hanson, "The Little Flower's Lisieux," October 1, 2020, *National Catholic Register*, https://www.ncregister.com/features/the-little-flower-s-lisieux.
3. *Soeur Thérèse of Lisieux, the Little Flower of Jesus: A New and Complete Translation of L'Histoire D'Une Ame, with an Account of Some Favours Attributed to the Intercession of Soeur Thérèse*, ed. T. N. Taylor (London: Burns, Oates & Washbourne, 1922), chapter 2, "A Catholic Household."

to and love for God grew, she also struggled with an excessively guilty conscience, which she called "scruples." She experienced further emotional pain due to separation when her two oldest sisters, Pauline and Marie, who had been mother figures to her, eventually entered the Carmelite convent in Lisieux.

Thérèse considered December 25, 1886, a week before her fourteenth birthday, to be the day of her "complete conversion" and release when God healed her within. After she had struggled with feelings of loss, inadequacy, and extreme sensitiveness for close to a decade, "in an instant, our Lord, satisfied with my good will, accomplished the work I had not been able to do during all these years.… Love and a spirit of self-forgetfulness took possession of me."[4]

Desiring to devote her life completely to God, and with her father's approval, she sought to join the Carmelite convent at the age of fifteen, but the religious authorities were unwilling to consent. During a pilgrimage to Rome, which included a general audience with the pope, she pleaded with the pontiff to grant her request. Although she did not receive the pope's permission, the bishop of the local diocese agreed shortly thereafter.

Thérèse considered herself a "little flower" of Jesus—obscure as a blossom in God's field, but delighted in and cared for by Him. She was fully committed to the exacting lifestyle of the Carmelite order, but, as she endeavored to live in full obedience and surrender to God, she found herself unable "to climb the steep stairway of perfection." She sought a simpler, scriptural way to reach God, eventually recognizing that she needed to remain

---

4. *Soeur Thérèse of Lisieux*, chapter 5, "Vocation of Thérèse."

"little" and allow Jesus to "lift" her to God and enable her to love and obey Him. The "little way" she discovered—that of humility, trust, sacrifice, and resting in God's deep love—captured the essence of the gospel with profound simplicity. It transformed her relationship with her heavenly Father, and its ripple effects have surged to a global impact that continues to this day.

Thérèse experienced spiritual dryness and temptations against faith, and she also contracted tuberculosis, from which she suffered greatly, but she strongly held on to her lifelong love of God. The doctor who attended her said, "I have never seen anyone suffer so intensely with such a look of supernatural joy."[5] Before her death on September 30, 1897, Thérèse wrote three accounts of various aspects of her life and spirituality that were posthumously published together as her autobiography under the title *The Story of a Soul*. The book, which included her deep insights into "the little way" and other spiritual matters, was immediately popular and eventually became a worldwide bestseller, with millions of copies in print. The work has been translated into more than sixty languages and dialects.

Thérèse was canonized by the Roman Catholic Church on May 17, 1925, and was declared a doctor of the Church on October 19, 1997. Pope Pius X called her "the greatest saint of modern times," and Pope John Paul II described her insights into faith as "vast and profound." Followers of Thérèse's little way transcend denominational boundaries, and her words and way of life continue to inspire millions.

---

5. *Soeur Thérèse of Lisieux*, "Epilogue: A Victim of Divine Love."

# *little flowers*
# in GOD's Field

Our Lord…showed me the book of nature, and I understood that every flower created by Him is beautiful, that the brilliance of the rose and the whiteness of the lily do not lessen the perfume of the violet or the sweet simplicity of the daisy. I understood that if all the lowly flowers wished to be roses, nature would lose its springtide beauty, and the fields would no longer be enameled with lovely hues. And so it is in the world of souls, our Lord's living garden. He has been pleased to create great saints who may be compared to the lily and the rose, but He has also created lesser ones who must be content to be daisies or simple violets flowering at His feet, and whose mission it is to gladden His divine eyes when He deigns to look down on them. And the more gladly they do His will, the greater is their perfection.

I understood this, also: that God's love is made manifest as well in a simple soul that does not resist His grace as in one more highly endowed. In fact, the characteristic of love being self-abasement, if all souls resembled the holy doctors who have illuminated the church, it seems that God, in coming to them, would not stoop low enough. But He has created the little child who knows nothing and can but utter feeble cries, and the [uncultivated person] who has only the natural law to guide him, and it is to their hearts that He deigns to stoop. These are the field flowers whose simplicity charms Him; and, by His condescension to them, our Savior shows His infinite greatness. As the sun shines both on the cedar and on the floweret, so the divine Sun illumines every soul, great and small, and all correspond to His care—just as in nature the seasons are so disposed that on the appointed day the humblest daisy shall unfold its petals.

## the little way of St. Thérèse

It has ever been my desire to become a saint, but I have always felt, in comparing myself with the saints, that I am as far removed from them as the grain of sand that the passerby tramples underfoot is remote from the mountain whose summit is lost in the clouds.

Instead of being discouraged, I concluded that God would not inspire desires that could not be realized, and that I may aspire to sanctity in spite of my littleness. For me to become great is impossible. I must bear with myself and my many imperfections; but I will seek out a means of getting to heaven by a little way—very short and very straight—a little way that is wholly new. We live in an age of inventions. Nowadays, the rich need not trouble to climb the stairs; they have lifts instead. Well, I mean to try and find a lift by which I may be raised to God, for I am too tiny to climb the steep stairway of perfection. I have sought

to find in Holy Scripture some suggestion as to what this lift might be that I so much desired, and I read these words uttered by the Eternal Wisdom Itself: "Whosoever is a little one, let him come to Me."* Then I drew near to God, feeling sure that I had discovered what I sought; but wishing to know further what He would do to the little one, I continued my search, and this is what I found: "You shall be carried at the breasts and upon the knees; as one whom the mother caresseth, so will I comfort you."**

Never have I been consoled by words more tender and sweet. Your arms, then, O Jesus, are the lift that must raise me up even to heaven. To get there, I need not grow. On the contrary, I must remain little; I must become still less.

*Proverbs 9:4.
**See Isaiah 66:12–13.

When Thérèsè was asked, "What is this little way that you would teach to souls?" this was her reply:

It is the way of spiritual childhood, the way of trust and absolute self-surrender.

I want to point out to them the means that I have always found so perfectly successful, to tell them that there is but one thing to do here below: we must offer Jesus the flowers of little sacrifices and win Him by a caress. That is how I have won Him, and that is why I shall be made so welcome.

*I am a very little soul who can offer only very little things to our Lord. It still happens that I frequently let slip the occasion of these slender sacrifices, which bring so much peace. But this does not discourage me; I bear the loss of a little peace, and I try to be more watchful in the future.*

"Remaining little" means to recognize one's nothingness, to await everything from the goodness of God, to avoid being too much troubled at our faults; finally, not to worry over amassing spiritual riches, not to be solicitous about anything. Even among the poor, while a child is still small, he is given what is necessary; but, once he is grown up, his father will no longer feed him, and tells him to seek work and support himself. Well, it was to avoid hearing this that I have never wished to grow up, for I feel incapable of earning my livelihood, which is life eternal!

*O Sun, my only love, I am happy to feel myself
so small, so frail,
in Your sunshine, and I am in peace.*

Far from resembling those beautiful souls who have practiced all sorts of mortifications from their infancy, I made mine consist in simply checking my inclinations, keeping back an impatient answer, doing little services to those around me without setting store thereby, and a hundred other things of the kind.

*Our Lord made me understand that the only true glory is that which lasts forever; and that, to attain it, there is no need to do brilliant deeds but rather to hide from the eyes of others, and even from oneself, so that "the left hand does not know what the right hand does."\**

*See Matthew 6:3.

You tell me that you feel your weakness, but that is a grace. It is our Lord who sows the seeds of distrust of self in your soul. Do not be afraid! If you do not fail to give Him pleasure in small things, He will be obliged to help you in great ones.

Jesus does not ask for great deeds but only for gratitude and self-surrender....

This is all our Lord claims from us. He has need of our love—He has no need of our works.

I wish to give all to Jesus because He makes me understand that He alone is perfect happiness. All!—all shall be for Him! And even when I have nothing…, I will give Him this nothing.

You tell me you wish to see the fruit of your efforts. That is exactly what Jesus would hide from you. He likes to contemplate by Himself these little fruits of our virtue. They console Him.

[In preparation for my first Communion, my sister] Pauline taught me that I must...stir up in my heart fresh transports of love and fill it anew with flowers. Every day, therefore, I made a number of little sacrifices and acts of love which were to be transformed into so many flowers; violets or roses, cornflowers, daisies or forget-me-nots—in a word, all nature's blossoms were to form within me a cradle for the Holy Child.*

*CLFW, 31–32.

*Our Lord is often pleased to give*
*wisdom to little ones.*

Remember that He did not say, "I am the flower of the gardens, a carefully-tended rose" but "I am the flower of the fields and the lily of the valleys."* Well, you must always be as a drop of dew hidden in the heart of this beautiful Lily of the valley.

The dewdrop—what could be simpler, what more pure? It is not the child of the clouds; it is born beneath the starry sky and survives but a night. When the sun darts forth its ardent rays, the delicate pearls adorning each blade of grass quickly pass into the lightest of vapor....

Happy dewdrop, known to God alone, think not of the rushing torrents of this world! Envy not even the crystal stream that winds among the meadows. The ripple of its waters is sweet, indeed, but it can be heard by creatures. Besides, the field flower could never contain it in its cup. One must be so little to draw near to Jesus, and few are the souls that aspire to be little and unknown. "Are not the river and the brook," they urge, "of more use than a dewdrop? Of what avail is it? Its only purpose is to refresh for one moment some poor little field flower."

Ah! They little know the true Flower of the field. If they knew Him, they would understand better our Lord's reproach to Martha. Our Beloved needs neither our brilliant deeds nor our beautiful thoughts. If He were in search of lofty ideas, has He not His angels, whose knowledge infinitely surpasses that of the greatest genius of earth? Neither intellect nor other talents has He come to seek among us.… He has become the Flower of the field to show how much He loves simplicity.

*Song of Solomon 2:1.

When a gardener gives special attention to a fruit that he wishes to ripen early, he does so not with a view to leaving it on the tree but in order to place it on a well-spread table. Our Lord lavished His favors on His Little Flower in the same way. He wishes His mercies to shine forth in me—He who, while on earth, cried out in a transport of joy, "I bless Thee, O Father, because Thou hast hidden these things from the wise and prudent and hast revealed them to little ones."*

*Luke 10:21.

*Truly, the divine Heart's goodness and merciful love are*
*little known! It is true that to enjoy these treasures,*
*we must humble ourselves, must confess our nothingness…*
*and here is where many a soul draws back.*

Let us make of our heart a garden of delights where our sweet Savior may come and take His rest. Let us plant only lilies there, and sing with St. John of the Cross:

> There I remained in deep oblivion,
> My head reposing upon Him I love,
> Lost to myself and all!
> I cast my cares away and let them,
> heedless, mid the lilies lie.

*Do not forget that Jesus is All. You have only to lose
your own nothingness in that infinite All, and thereafter to
think only of that All who alone is worthy of your love.*

Just as a torrent carries into the depths of the sea all that it meets on its way, so, my Jesus, does the soul who plunges into the shoreless ocean of Your love bring with it all its treasures.

*O Jesus, I ask but peace....*
*Peace and, above all, love....*
*Love—without limit.*

O eternal Word! O my Savior! You are the divine Eagle whom I love—who lures me. You who, descending to this land of exile, did will to suffer and to die in order to bear away the souls of men and plunge them into the very heart of the blessed Trinity—love's eternal home!

*To be a true victim of Love,*
*we must surrender ourselves entirely....*
*Love will consume us only in the measure of*
*our self-surrender.*

[When I was a child, the kaleidoscope] excited my admiration, and I wondered what could provide so charming a phenomenon when, one day, after a lengthy examination, I found that it consisted simply of tiny bits of paper and cloth scattered inside. A further examination revealed that there were three mirrors inside the tube, and the problem was solved. It became for me the illustration of a great truth.

So long as our actions, even the most trivial, remain within Love's kaleidoscope, so long the Blessed Trinity, figured by the three mirrors, imparts to them a wonderful brightness and beauty. The eyepiece is Jesus Christ, and He, looking from outside through Himself into the kaleidoscope, finds perfect all our works. But if we leave that ineffable abode of Love, He would see but the rags and chaff of unclean and worthless deeds.

I asked Jesus to draw me into the fire of His love and to unite me so closely to Himself that He may live and act in me. I feel that the more the fire of love consumes my heart, so much the more I shall say, "Draw me!" and the more also will souls who draw near me run swiftly in the sweet fragrance of the Beloved.*

*See Song of Solomon 1:3–4.

*I had to pass through many trials before reaching the
haven of peace, before tasting the delicious fruits of perfect
love and of complete abandonment to God's will.*

It seems to me that God has no need of years to perfect His labor of love in a soul. One ray from His heart can in an instant make His flower blossom forth, never to fade.

*Love can take the place of a long life. Jesus does not consider
time, for He is eternal. He only looks at the love....
I do not desire the thrill of love that I can feel; if Jesus feels
its thrill, then that is enough for me. It is so sweet to love
Him, to make Him loved.*

To me, He has given His infinite mercy, and it is in this ineffable mirror that I contemplate His other attributes. Therein all appear to me radiant with love. His justice, even more perhaps than the rest, seems to me to be clothed with love. What joy to think that our Lord is just, that is to say, that He takes our weakness into account, that He knows perfectly the frailty of our nature! Of what, then, need I be afraid?

Will not the God of infinite justice, who deigns so lovingly to pardon the sins of the Prodigal Son, be also just to me "who am always with Him"?*

*See Luke 15:31.

*I cannot well see what more I shall have in heaven than I have now; I shall see God, it is true; but as to being with Him, I am already that, even on earth.*

The only way to advance rapidly in the path of love is to always remain very little. That is what I did, and now I can sing with our holy father, St. John of the Cross:

> Then I abased myself so low, so very low, that I ascended to such heights, such heights, indeed, that I did overtake the prey I chased!

*Among the disciples of the world, He meets with nothing*
*but indifference and ingratitude, and alas!*
*among His own, how few hearts surrender themselves*
*without reserve to the infinite tenderness of His love.*

How can a soul so imperfect as mine aspire to the plenitude of love? Why do You not reserve these infinite longings to lofty souls, to the eagles that soar in the heights? Alas! I am but a poor little unfledged bird. I am not an eagle; I have but the eagle's eyes and heart! Yet, notwithstanding my exceeding littleness, I dare to gaze upon the divine Sun of Love, and I burn to dart upward to Him! I would fly, I would imitate the eagles, but all that I can do is to lift up my little wings—it is beyond my feeble power to soar. What is to become of me? Must I die of sorrow because of my helplessness? Oh, no! I will not even grieve. With daring self-abandonment, I will remain there until death, my gaze fixed upon that divine Sun. Nothing shall frighten me, neither wind nor rain. And should impenetrable clouds conceal the Orb of Love, and should I seem to believe that beyond this life there is darkness only, that would be the hour of perfect joy, the hour in which to push my confidence to its uttermost bounds. I would not dare to detach my gaze, well knowing that beyond the dark clouds the sweet Sun still shines.

My God, You know that I have always desired to love You alone. It has been my only ambition. Your love has gone before me, even from the days of my childhood. It has grown with my growth, and now it is an abyss whose depths I cannot fathom.

Love attracts love; mine darts toward You and would desire to make the abyss brim over, but alas! it is not even as a dewdrop in the ocean. To love You as You love me, I must make Your love my own. In this way alone can I find rest.

*In heaven, God will do all I desire because, on earth,*
*I have never done my own will.*

How sweet was the first embrace of Jesus! It was indeed an embrace of love. I felt that I was loved, and I said, "I love You, and I give myself to You forever." Jesus asked nothing of me and claimed no sacrifice. For a long time, He and little Thérèse had known and understood one another. That day, our meeting was more than simple recognition; it was perfect union. We were no longer two. Thérèse had disappeared like a drop of water lost in the immensity of the ocean; Jesus alone remained—He was the Master, the King!

*To love You, Jesus, is now my only desire.*
*Great deeds are not for me; I cannot preach the gospel or*
*shed my blood. No matter! My brothers work in my stead,*
*and I, a little child, stay close to the throne and love*
*You for all who are in the strife.*

A few days after the oblation of myself to God's merciful love, I was in the choir, beginning the Way of the Cross, when I felt myself suddenly wounded by a dart of fire so ardent that I thought I would die. I do not know how to explain this transport; there is no comparison to describe the intensity of that flame. It seemed as though an invisible force plunged me wholly into fire.... But oh! what fire! what sweetness!

*Love can do all things. The most impossible tasks seem
to it easy and sweet. You know well that our Lord does not
look so much at the greatness of our actions, nor even at
their difficulty, as at the love with which we do them.*

You ask me for a method of obtaining perfection. I know of love—and love only! Our hearts are made for this alone. Sometimes I endeavor to find some other word for love, but in a land of exile, "words which have a beginning and an end"* are quite unable to render adequately the emotions of the soul, and so we must keep to the one simple word—LOVE.

But on whom shall our poor hearts lavish this love, and who will be worthy of this treasure? Is there anyone who will understand it, and—above all—is there anyone who will be able to repay?... Jesus alone understands love; He alone can give back all—yes, infinitely more than the utmost we can give.

*St. Augustine.

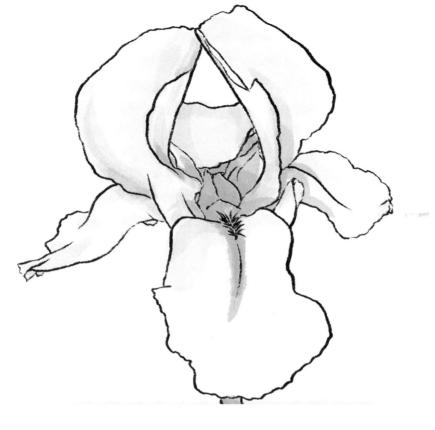

*If, supposing the impossible, God Himself could not*
*see my good actions, I would not be troubled.*
*I love Him so much that I would like to give Him joy*
*without His knowing who gave it.*

Which Thérèse will be the more fervent?…
She who will be the more humble, the more
closely united to Jesus, and the more faithful in making love the mainspring of every
action. We must not let slip one single occasion of sacrifice, everything has such value
in the religious life.… Pick up a pin from a
motive of love, and you may thereby convert
a soul. Jesus alone can make our deeds of
such worth, so let us love Him with every
fiber of our heart.

*Do not fear to tell Jesus that you love Him,*
*even though you may not feel that love. In this way,*
*you will compel Him to come to your aid and to carry you*
*like a little child who is too weak to walk.*

Our Lord, whose heart is always watching, taught me that He granted miracles to those whose faith is as small as a grain of mustard seed, in the hope of strengthening this slender faith, while, for His intimate friends, for His mother, He did not work miracles till He had proved their faith. Did He not permit Lazarus to die even though Mary and Martha had sent word that he was sick? And at the marriage feast of Cana, when Our Lady asked her divine Son to aid the master of the house, did He not answer that His hour had not yet come? But after the trial, what a reward! Water is changed into wine,* and Lazarus rises from the dead.**

*See John 2:1–11.
**See John 11:1–45.

*From Your adorable lips, we have heard Your loving plaint,
"I thirst."\* Since we know that this thirst that consumes
You is a thirst for love, to quench it, we would wish to
possess an infinite love.*

\*See John 19:28.

Jesus is content with a tender look or a sigh of love. For my part, I find it quite easy to practice perfection, now that I realize it only means making Jesus captive through His heart. Look at a little child who has just vexed its mother, either by giving way to temper or by disobedience. If it hides in a corner and is sulky, or if it cries for fear of being punished, its mother will certainly not forgive the fault. But should it run to her with its little arms outstretched and say, "Kiss me, Mother; I will not do it again!" what mother would not straightway clasp her child lovingly to her heart and forget all it had done?... She knows quite well that her little one will repeat the fault—no matter, her darling will escape all punishment as long as it makes appeal to her heart....

Let us learn to keep Him prisoner—this God, the divine Beggar of Love.... He shows us that the smallest actions done for His love are those that charm His heart. If it were necessary to do great things, we should be deserving of pity; but we are happy beyond measure because Jesus lets Himself be led captive by the smallest action.

As our Lord is now in heaven, I can only follow Him by the footprints He has left— footprints full of life, full of fragrance. I have only to open the Holy Gospels, and at once I breathe the perfume of Jesus, and then I know which way to run; and it is not to the first place, but to the last, that I hasten. I leave the Pharisee to go up, and, full of confidence, I repeat the humble prayer of the publican. Above all, I follow Magdalene, for the amazing—rather, I should say, the loving— audacity that delights the heart of Jesus has cast its spell upon mine. It is not because I have been preserved from mortal sin that I lift up my heart to God in trust and love. I feel that even if I had on my conscience every crime one could commit, I would lose nothing of my confidence. My heart broken with sorrow, I would throw myself into the arms of my Savior. I know that He loves the Prodigal Son; I have heard His words to St. Mary Magdalene, to the woman taken in adultery, and to the woman of Samaria. No one could frighten me, for I know what to believe concerning His mercy and His love. And I know that all that multitude of sins would disappear in an instant, even as a drop of water cast into a flaming furnace.

[Ever] since I...have been given to understand the love of the heart of Jesus, I confess that all fear has been driven from mine. The remembrance of my faults humbles me; and it helps me never to rely upon my own strength—which is but weakness—but, more than all, it speaks to me of mercy and of love. When a soul with childlike trust casts her faults into Love's all-devouring furnace, how shall they escape being utterly consumed?

*I have never given the good God anything but love.*
*It is with love He will repay.*

The only way I have of proving my love is to strew flowers before You—that is to say, I will let no tiny sacrifice pass, no look, no word. I wish to profit by the smallest actions and to do them for love. I wish to suffer for love's sake, and for love's sake even to rejoice; thus shall I strew flowers. Not one shall I find without scattering its petals before You… and I will sing…I will sing always, even if my roses must be gathered from amid thorns; and the longer and sharper the thorns, the sweeter shall be my song.

*It seems to me that if our sacrifices take Jesus captive, our joys make Him prisoner too. All that is needed to attain this end is that, instead of giving ourselves over to selfish happiness, we offer to our Spouse the little joys He scatters in our path to charm our hearts and draw them toward Him.*

Meditating on the mystical body of holy church, I could not recognize myself among any of its members as described by St. Paul, or was it not rather that I wished to recognize myself in all? Charity provided me with the key to my vocation. I understood that since the church is a body composed of different members, the noblest and most important of all the organs would not be lacking.... I understood that love embraces all vocations, that it is all things, and that it reaches out through all the ages and to the uttermost limits of the earth because it is eternal.

Then, beside myself with joy, I cried out, "O Jesus, my Love, at last I have found my vocation. My vocation is love! Yes, I have found my place in the bosom of the church, and this place, O my God, You Yourself have given to me. In the heart of the church, my mother, I will be LOVE!... Thus I shall be all things: thus will my dream be realized."...

I am but a weak and helpless child, yet it is my very weakness that makes me dare to offer myself, O Jesus, as victim to Your love.

I had never before fathomed these words of our Lord: "The second commandment is like to the first: Thou shalt love thy neighbour as thyself."* I had set myself above all to love God, and it was in loving Him that I discovered the hidden meaning of these other words: "It is not those who say, Lord, Lord! who enter into the kingdom of heaven, but he who does the will of My Father."**...

...I know now that true charity consists in bearing all our neighbors' defects—not being surprised at their weakness but edified at their smallest virtues.

*Matthew 22:39.
**See Matthew 7:21.

*Jesus, Jesus! If the mere desire of Your love awakens such delight, what will it be to possess it, to enjoy it forever?*

It may be that, someday, my present state will appear to me full of defects, but nothing now surprises me, and I do not even distress myself that I am so weak. On the contrary, I glory in it and expect to find fresh imperfections each day. No, I must confess, these lights [revelations] on my own nothingness are of more good to my soul than lights on matters of faith. Remembering that "charity covereth a multitude of sins,"* I draw from this rich mine that our Savior has opened to us in the Gospels. I search the depths of His adorable words and cry out with David, "I have run in the way of Thy commandments, since Thou hast enlarged my heart."** And charity alone can make the heart wide. O Jesus! Since its sweet flame consumes my heart, I run with delight in the way of Your new commandment.***

*1 Peter 4:8.
**See Psalm 119:32.
***See John 13:34.

*I know [that] when I show charity to others,
it is simply Jesus acting in me, and the more closely I am
united to Him, the more dearly I love my Sisters.*

He wishes me to love Him because He has forgiven me not only much but everything. Without waiting for me to love Him much, as St. Mary Magdalene did,* He has made me understand how He has loved me with an indescribable love and forethought, so that now my love may know no bounds.

*How can a heart given up to human affections be closely
united to God? It seems to me that it is impossible. I have seen
so many souls, allured by this false light like poor moths, fly
right into it, burn their wings, and then return wounded to
our Lord, the divine Fire that burns but does not consume.*

Fully sweet is the way of love. It is true one may fall and be unfaithful to grace; but love, knowing how to profit by everything, quickly consumes whatever is displeasing to Jesus, leaving in the heart only a deep and humble peace.

*Because [my heart] has loved [God] only, it has grown,
little by little, and now it can give to those who are
dear to Him a far deeper and truer love than if it were
centered in a barren and selfish affection.*

Truly, in prayer and sacrifice lie all my strength; they are my invincible arms. Experience has taught me that they touch hearts far more easily than words....

How wonderful is the power of prayer! It is like a queen, who, having free access to the king, obtains whatsoever she asks....

...I do as children who have not learned to read—I simply tell our Lord all that I want, and He always understands.

With me, prayer is an uplifting of the heart, a glance toward heaven, a cry of gratitude and love uttered equally in sorrow and in joy. In a word, it is something noble, supernatural, that expands my soul and unites it to God.

*[I have many distractions during prayer], but as soon as I am aware of them, I pray for those people the thought of whom is diverting my attention, and in this way they reap benefit from my distractions.*

"Give me a lever and a fulcrum on which to lean it," said Archimedes, "and I will lift the world."

What he could not obtain because his request had only a material end, without reference to God, the saints have obtained in all its fullness. They lean on God Almighty's power itself, and their lever is the prayer that inflames with love's fire. With this lever, they have raised the world.

*I have often observed that our Lord will not give me any store of provisions but instead nourishes me each moment with food that is ever new; I find it within me without knowing how it has come there. I simply believe that it is Jesus Himself, hidden in my poor heart, who is secretly at work, inspiring me with what He wishes me to do as each occasion arises.*

Some time ago, I was watching the flicker, almost invisible, of a tiny night-light, when one of the Sisters drew near and, lighting her candle in the dying flame, passed it round to light all those of the Community. "Who dare glory in his own good works?" I reflected. "From one faint spark such as this, it would be possible to set the whole earth on fire." We often think we receive graces and are divinely illumined by means of brilliant candles. But where does their light come from? From the prayers, perhaps, of some humble, hidden soul whose inward shining is not apparent to human eyes, a soul of unrecognized virtue and, in her own sight, of little value—a dying flame.

What mysteries will yet be unveiled to us! I have often thought that perhaps I owe all the graces with which I am laden to some little soul whom I shall know only in heaven.…

And do you not think that the great saints, on their side, seeing what they owe to all little souls, will love them with a love beyond compare? The friendships of paradise will be both sweet and full of surprise, of this I am certain. The familiar friend of an apostle or of a great doctor of the church may be a shepherd boy, and a simple little child may be united in closest intimacy with a patriarch.… I long to enter that kingdom of love!

Lately, I have been thinking what I could undertake for the salvation of souls, and these simple words of the gospel have given me light. Pointing to the fields of ripe corn, Jesus once said to His disciples, "Lift up your eyes and see the fields, for they are already white with the harvest";* and again: "The harvest indeed is great, but the labourers are few; pray ye therefore the Lord of the harvest that He send forth labourers."**

Here is a mystery indeed! Is not Jesus all-powerful? Do not creatures belong to Him who made them? Why does He deign to say, "Pray ye the Lord of the harvest that He send forth laborers"? It is because His love for us is so unsearchable, so tender, that He wishes us to share in all He does. The Creator of the universe awaits the prayer of a poor little soul to save a multitude of other souls, ransomed, like her, at the price of His blood.

*John 4:35.
**Matthew 9:37–38.

It is from the Gospels that I find most help in the time of prayer; from them, I draw all that I need for my poor soul. I am always discovering in them new lights and hidden mysterious meanings. I know, and I have experienced, that "the kingdom of God is within us."* Our Lord has no need of books or teachers to instruct our souls. He, the Teacher of teachers, instructs us without any noise of words. I have never heard Him speak, yet I know He is within me. He is there, always guiding and inspiring me; and just when I need them, lights, hitherto unseen, break in. This is not, as a rule, during my prayers but in the midst of my daily duties.

*See Luke 17:21.

*You want to climb the mountain,*
*whereas God wishes you to descend it. He is awaiting you*
*in the fruitful valley of humility.*

Our Lord also taught me, "Give to everyone that asketh thee; and of him that taketh away thy goods, ask them not again."* To give to everyone who asks is not as pleasant as to give of one's own accord. If we are asked pleasantly, it is easy to give; but if we are asked discourteously, then, unless we are perfect in charity, there is an inward rebellion, and we find no end of excuses for refusing.... And if it is difficult to give to whoever asks, it is far more difficult to let what belongs to us be taken without our asking for it back.... I say this is hard, but I should rather say that it seems hard, for "the yoke of the Lord is sweet and His burden light."** And when we submit to that yoke, we at once feel its sweetness.

*Luke 6:30.
**Matthew 11:30.

*I know that by humility alone can saints be made, and I also know that our trial is a mine of gold for us to turn to account. I, who am but a little grain of sand, wish to set to work, though I have neither courage nor strength. Now, this very lack of power will make my task easier, for I wish to work for love.*

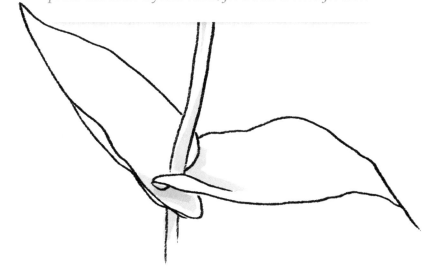

The one thing that is not open to envy is the lowest place. Here alone, therefore, there is neither vanity nor affliction of spirit. Yet "the way of a man is not his own,"* and sometimes we find ourselves wishing for what dazzles. In that hour, let us in all humility take our place among the imperfect and look upon ourselves as little souls who, at every instant, need to be upheld by the goodness of God. From the moment He sees us fully convinced of our nothingness and hears us cry out, "My foot stumbles, Lord, but Thy mercy is my strength,"** He reaches out His hand to us. But, should we attempt great things, even under pretext of zeal, He deserts us. It suffices, therefore, to humble ourselves, to bear with meekness our imperfections. Herein lies—for us—true holiness.

*Jeremiah 10:23.
**Psalm 94:18.

*Since I have abandoned all thought of self-seeking,*
*I live the happiest life possible.*

If the apostle [Peter] had caught some small fish, perhaps our divine Master would not have worked a miracle; but he had caught nothing, and so, through the power and goodness of God, his nets were soon filled with great fishes.* Such is our Lord's way. He gives as God—with divine largesse—but He insists on humility of heart.

**See Luke 5:1–11.

*True greatness is not found in a name*
*but in the soul.*

If, for example, I were to say, "I have acquired such and such a virtue, and I can practice it"; or again, "My God, You know I love You too much to dwell on one single thought against faith," straightway I would be assailed by the most dangerous temptations and would certainly yield. To prevent this misfortune, I have but to say humbly and from my heart, "My God, I beseech You not to let me be unfaithful."

I understand clearly how St. Peter fell. He placed too much reliance on his own ardent nature instead of leaning solely on the divine strength. Had he only said, "Lord, give me strength to follow You unto death," the grace would not have been refused him.

*My God, I choose everything; I will not be a saint by halves. I am not afraid of suffering for You. I only fear one thing, and that is to do my own will. Accept the offering of my will, for I choose all that You will.*

What pleases Jesus in my little soul is to see me love my littleness and to see my blind trust in His Mercy. Because I was little and weak Jesus stooped down to me and tenderly instructed me in the secrets of His love. It was Jesus who did all in me, and I—I did nothing but be little and weak.*

*CLFW*, 52.

*I used to ask myself how, in days to come, I could
more clearly understand the true meaning of perfection.
At that time, I imagined I understood it completely, but I
soon came to realize that the more one advances along this
path, the farther one seems from the goal, and now I am
resigned always to be imperfect, and I even find joy in that.*

How happy does our Lord make me, and how sweet and easy is His service on this earth! He has always given me what I desired, or rather He has made me desire what He wishes to give. A short time before my terrible temptation against faith, I had reflected how few exterior trials, worthy of mention, had fallen to my lot, and that if I were to have interior trials, God must change my path; and this I did not think He would do. Yet I could not always live at ease. Of what means, then, would He make use?

I did not have long to wait for an answer, and it showed me that He whom I love is never at a loss, for, without changing my way, He sent me this great trial; and thus mingled a healing bitterness with all the sweet.

Sometimes, when I read books in which perfection is put before us with the goal obstructed by a thousand obstacles, my poor little head is quickly fatigued. I close the learned treatise, which tires my brain and dries up my heart, and I turn to the sacred Scriptures. Then all becomes clear and lightsome—a single word opens out infinite vistas, perfection appears easy, and I see that it is enough to acknowledge our nothingness and, like children, surrender ourselves into the arms of the good God. Leaving to great and lofty minds the beautiful books that I cannot understand, still less put into practice, I rejoice in my littleness because "only little children and those who are like them shall be admitted to the heavenly banquet."*

*See Matthew 18:3; 19:14.

Dear Lord, You know my weakness. Each morning, I resolve to be humble, and in the evening, I recognize that I have often been guilty of pride. The sight of these faults tempts me to discouragement; yet I know that discouragement is itself but a form of pride. I wish, therefore, O my God, to build all my trust upon You. As You can do all things, deign to implant in my soul this virtue that I desire; and to obtain it from Your infinite mercy, I will often say to You, "Jesus, meek and humble of heart, make my heart like Yours."

*I wish to be holy, but, knowing how helpless I am,*
*I beseech You, my God, to be Yourself my holiness.*

I am too little now to be guilty of vanity; I am likewise too little to endeavor to prove my humility by fine-sounding words. I prefer to admit in all simplicity that "He who is mighty has done great things for me"*— and the greatest is that He has shown me my littleness and how incapable I am of anything good.

*See Luke 1:49.

It pleases Jesus to lavish His gifts on certain souls in order to draw yet others to Himself. In His mercy, He humbles them inwardly and gently compels them to recognize their nothingness and His almighty power. Now, this sentiment of humility is like a kernel of grace that God hastens to develop against that blessed day when, clothed with an imperishable beauty, they will be placed, without danger, on the banqueting table of paradise.

You must practice the little virtues. This is sometimes difficult, but God never refuses the first grace—courage for self-conquest; and if the soul corresponds to that grace, she at once finds herself in God's sunlight.... In the onset, we must act with courage. By this means, the heart gains strength, and victory follows victory.

*Honors are always dangerous.*
*What poisonous food is served daily to those in high*
*positions! What deadly fumes of incense! A soul must be well*
*detached from herself to pass unscathed through it all.*

In this world, there is no fruitfulness without suffering—either physical pain, secret sorrow, or trials known sometimes only to God. When good thoughts and generous resolutions have sprung up in our souls through reading the lives of the saints, we should not content ourselves, as in the case of secular books, with paying a certain tribute of admiration to the genius of their authors. Rather, we should consider the price they have doubtless paid for that supernatural good they have produced.

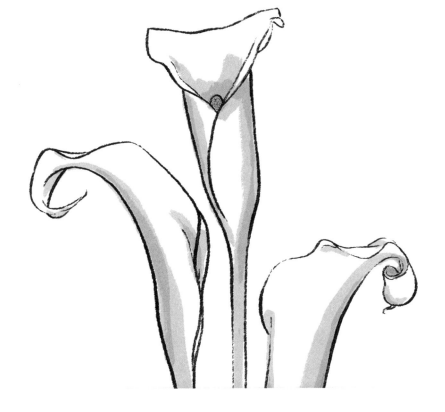

*To me it seems that humility is truth.*

Believe me, the writing of pious books, the composing of the sublimest poetry, all that does not equal the smallest act of self-denial.

There are people who make the worst of everything. As for me, I do just the contrary. I always see the good side of things, and even if my portion is suffering, without a glimmer of solace, well, I make it my joy.

To scatter flowers!—that means each sacrifice:
   My lightest sighs and pains, my heaviest, saddest
      hours,
My hopes, my joys, my prayers—I will not count
   the price—
   Behold my flowers!

With deep untold delight Your beauty fills my
   soul,
   Would I might light this love in hearts of all
      who live!
For this, my fairest flowers, all things in my
   control,
   How fondly, gladly would I give!…

To scatter flowers!—that means, to speak of
   You—
   My only pleasure here, where tears fill all the
      hours;
But soon, with angel hosts, my spirit shall be free
   To scatter flowers.

If I had been rich, I never could have seen a poor person hungry without giving him something to eat. This is also my way in the spiritual life. There are many souls on the brink of hell, and as my earnings come to hand, they are scattered among these sinners. The time has never yet been when I could say, "Now I am going to work for myself."

*All is well when one seeks only
the Master's will.*

For years, I have not belonged to myself. I have surrendered myself wholly to Jesus, and He is free to do with me whatsoever He pleases.

I find that trials are a great help toward detachment from the things of earth: they make one look higher than this world. Nothing here can satisfy, and we can find rest only in holding ourselves ready to do God's will.

We can never have too much confidence in
the good God; He is so mighty, so merciful.
As we hope in Him, so shall we receive.

My Heaven is—to feel in me the likeness

Of the God of power who created me;

My Heaven is—to stay forever in His
presence,

To call Him Father—just His child to be;

*Safe in His Arms* divine, near to His sacred
Face,

Resting upon His Heart, of the storm I
have no fear;

*Abandonment* complete, this is my only
law—

Behold my Heaven Here!*

*CLFW, 57.

Life is not dreary; on the contrary, it is most joyful. Now, if you said, "Exile [our existence on earth] is dreary," I could understand. It is a mistake to call "life" that which must have an end. Such a word should be used only of the joys of heaven—joys that are unfading— and in this true meaning, life is not sad but joyful—most joyful.

I saw at a glance that the task was beyond my strength. Throwing myself without delay into our Lord's arms, I imitated those tiny children who, when they are frightened, hide their faces on their father's shoulder....

The knowledge that it was impossible to do anything of myself rendered my task easier. My one interior occupation was to unite myself more and more closely to God, knowing that the rest would be given to me over and above.

*It is wrong to pass one's time in fretting instead
of sleeping on the heart of Jesus.*

Life is often burdensome and bitter. It is painful to begin a day of toil, especially when Jesus hides Himself from our love. What is this sweet Friend about? Does He not see our anguish and the burden that weighs us down? Why does He not come and comfort us?

Be not afraid.... He is here at hand.... I assure you that it costs Him dear to fill us with bitterness, but He knows that it is the only means of preparing us to know Him as He knows Himself, and to become ourselves divine! Our soul is indeed great, and our destiny glorious. Let us lift ourselves above all things that pass and hold ourselves far from the earth! Up above, the air is so pure.... Jesus may hide Himself, but we know that He is there.

*It is so sweet to serve God in the dark night
and in the midst of trial. After all, we have but this
life in which to live by faith.*

At the hour when the sun seems to sink into the vast ocean, leaving behind it a trail of glory, I sat with Pauline on a bare rock and gazed for a long while on this golden furrow, which she told me was an image of grace illumining the way of faithful souls here below. Then I pictured my soul as a tiny barque, with a graceful white sail, in the midst of the furrow, and I resolved never to let it withdraw from the sight of Jesus so that it might sail peacefully and quickly toward the heavenly shore.

When I am in this state of spiritual dryness, unable to pray or to practice virtue, I look for little opportunities, for the smallest trifles, to please my Jesus: a smile or a kind word, for instance, when I would wish to be silent or to show that I am bored. If no such occasion offers, I try at least to say over and over again that I love Him. This is not hard, and it keeps the fire in my heart alive. Even if the fire of love seems dead, I would still throw my tiny straws on the ashes, and I am confident it would light up again.

We who run in the way of love must never allow ourselves to be disturbed by anything. If I did not simply live from one moment to another, it would be impossible for me to be patient; but I only look at the present, I forget the past, and I take good care not to anticipate the future. When we yield to discouragement or despair, it is usually because we think too much about the past and the future.

*If you wish to be a saint—and it will not be hard—
keep only one end in view: give pleasure to
Jesus and bind yourself more closely to Him.*

There is but one thing to be done here below: to love Jesus and to save souls for Him, that He may be more loved. We must not let slip the smallest opportunity of giving Him joy. We must refuse Him nothing. He is in such need of love.

I see so many beautiful horizons, such infinitely varied tints, that the palette of the divine Painter alone will, after the darkness of this life, be able to supply me with the colors with which I may portray the wonders that my soul sees.

*Jesus!... Oh! I would so love Him!*
*Love Him as He has never yet been loved!*

When the evening of life comes, I shall stand before You with empty hands, because I do not ask You, my God, to take account of my works. All our works of righteousness are blemished in Your eyes.* I wish, therefore, to be robed with Your own righteousness, and to receive from Your love the everlasting gift of Yourself. I desire no other throne, no other crown, but You, O my Beloved!

*See Isaiah 64:6.

My longing will be the same in heaven as upon earth: to love Jesus and to make Him loved.